Sophie — May your day
brim with cuddles!
love mum
14.2.03

Shakespeare on ...
Love and Sex

Shakespeare on ...
Love and Sex

Katherine and
Elizabeth O'Mahoney

PRION

First published 2002 in Great Britain by
Prion Books Limited
Imperial Works, Perren Street
London NW5 3ED
www.prionbooks.com

Selection copyright © Katherine and
Elizabeth O'Mahoney 2002

ISBN 1-85375-497-8

Cover design by Grade Design Consultants
Printed and bound in Great Britain

Introduction

It is a well-known fact that the British do not have sex. Occasionally we might indulge in a little rumpy-pumpy, but the British never engage in sexual intercourse. We shrink from the word itself, preferring to use euphemism, pun and innuendo to describe the mechanics of reproductive goings-on.

Sixteenth-century England was not a nation to bandy around the 'S' word either. Instead, Shakespeare talks of 'the beast with two backs', 'exchanging the flesh' and, more curiously, 'hanging one's bugle in an invisible baldrick'.

But while Shakespeare shies away from the 'S' word, unlike many men, he shows no qualms in using the 'L' word. His plays and sonnets reveal a complete, colourful spectrum of amorous activities, from the macabre marriage of the Macbeths to the possessive passions of Antony and Cleopatra. This small tome, *Shakespeare On Love and Sex*, presents all that Shakespeare has to say about the sexual and spiritual sphere of love, from the saucy to the sublime, from the bawdy to the breathtaking.

Today, over 400 years after they were created, Romeo and Juliet are regarded as the greatest lovers of English literature. The fact that she is only thirteen and he old enough to know better, that they only knew each other two days and both end up dead, serves only to compound their iconic status. But whatever else the play shows us *Romeo and Juliet*, like much of the Bard's work, reminds us that love is never plain sailing. Shakespeare was only too familiar with the problems of love, and his plays frequently serve as a lesson in 'how not to do it'. Lovers fall victim to depression, insanity, suicide and murder. Furthermore, in a typical Shakespearean play, the lover will not only end up dead, but might also fall in love with a statue, nun, transvestite or, if you're really unlucky, a donkey.

Alternatively, a character might sleep with his brother's wife, an uncle, a sister or almost any member of the immediate family.

Shakespeare's lessons in love also extend to the mundane problems of the boudoir, which plagued Renaissance romantics as they do us today. Sixteenth-century self-help books offered handy hints on how women could achieve orgasm and overcome infertility. For randy Romeos there were a number of remedies to ensure male performance. 'Cockale' was an early prototype for Viagra, and as the name suggests, was made by boiling a rooster in ale. While momentarily disrupting the amorous ambience, a quick slug of Cockale would restore any Jacobean gigolo to his full sexual prowess. If that failed, however, a die-hard romantic could always try taking the powdered penis of a stag, a remedy suggested by Peltro Mattoli in the middle of the sixteenth century. Inspired by such paraphernalia, the Bawdy Bard depicts characters with textbook sexual difficulties: male characters worry over loss of erection, premature ejaculation and, of course, constantly fret over size.

And let's not forget the myriad of homosexual themes and images in Shakespeare. Although 'the detestable and abominable vice of buggery' was made illegal in 1533 Shakespeare, like many of the finest European writers and artists of the time, flouted this prejudice in quiet celebration of same-sex relationships. The notorious sonnet twenty, with its overt tones of homosexuality has been much debated since its publication.

But despite the complications of sex and love, William Shakespeare's plays present the timeless appeal of romance. From the Oedipus complex to cross dressing, the work of Shakespeare trawls the depths of human sexuality in a way that highlights both its intriguing fascination and its enduring innocence.

And so, with sweaty hands and a fluttering heart, let us peruse the enchanting entries of this modest collection, *Shakespeare on Love and Sex*, which is dedicated to Shakespeare's ageless insights into love, lust and what comes most naturally to all of us.

Katherine and Elizabeth O'Mahoney, 2002

Alas, that love, so
gentle in his view,
Should be so tyrannous
and rough in proof.

Romeo and Juliet 1.1.162-3

Men have died from time to time and worms have eaten them, but not for love.

As You Like it 4.1.91-2

He did love her, sir, as a
gentleman loves a woman...
He loved her, sir,
and loved her not.

All's Well That Ends Well. 5.3.247-9

Dumb jewels often in
their silent kind,
More than quick words,
do move a woman's mind.

The Two Gentlemen of Verona 3.1.90-1

Love is a smoke made
with the fume of sighs.

Romeo and Juliet 1.1.183

I'll make my heaven
in a lady's lap.

3 Henry VI 3.2.148

Lovers and madmen
have such seething brains
Such shaping fantasies,
that apprehend
More than cool
reason ever comprehends.

A Midsummer Night's Dream 5.1.4-6

The 24 clay pipes found near Shakespeare's Stratford home may have been used to smoke tobacco, marijuana or hallucinogenic drugs.

She will die if he love her not,
and she will die ere she make
her love known.

Much Ado About Nothing 2.3.156-8

You cannot call it love,
for at your age
The heyday in the
blood is tame.

Hamlet 3.4.67-8

For where thou art,
there is the world itself, ...
And where thou
art not, desolation.

2 Henry VI 3.2.364-6

Get thee to a nunnery.

Hamlet 3.1.122

In his will,
Shakespeare left his
wife their
'second-best bed'.

Love is a spirit all
compact of fire,
Not gross to sink, but light,
and will aspire.

Venus and Adonis 149-50

I pray you, do not
fall in love with me,
For I am falser than
vows made in wine.

As You Like It 3.5.73-4

It is a greater grief
To bear love's wrong,
than hate's known injury.

Sonnet 40

Come, woo me, woo me;
for I am in a holiday humour
and like enough to consent.

As You Like It 4.1.59-60

Love is not love
Which alters when
it alteration finds.

Sonnet 116

I would not wish
Any companion in
the world but you.

The Tempest 3.1.54-5

All theatres were destroyed in 1642 by order of Parliament.

Love sought is good, but given unsought is better.

Twelfth Night 3.1.147

O, they love least that let
men know their love.

The Two Gentlemen of Verona 1.2.32

I will live in thy heart, die in thy lap, and be buried in thy eyes. And moreover, I will go with thee to thy uncle's.

Much Ado About Nothing 5.2.86-7

Love is like a child
That longs for everything
that he can come by.

The Two Gentlemen of Verona 3.1.124-5

A replica of the Globe
Theatre was erected for the
Great Texas Fair in 1936.
Water from the river Avon
consecrated the new
American theatre.

These violent delights
have violent ends ...
Therefore, love moderately.

Romeo and Juliet 2.5.9-14

My Oberon! What
visions have I seen!
Methought I was
enamoured of an ass.

A Midsummer Night's Dream 4.1.73-4

What a pretty thing man
is when he goes in his
doublet and hose and
leaves off his wit!

Much Ado About Nothing 5.1.189-90

Doubt thou the stars are fire,
Doubt that the sun doth move,
Doubt truth to be a liar,
But never doubt I love.

Hamlet 2.2.116-9

I humbly do beseech
you of your pardon
For too much loving you.

Othello 3.3.216-7

Come what sorrow can,
It cannot countervail the
exchange of joy
That one short minute gives
me in her sight.

Romeo and Juliet 2.6.3-5

Shakespeare survived the Black Death. This epidemic killed over 33,000 in London alone in 1603.

Sigh no more, ladies,
sigh no more.
Men were deceivers ever.

Much Ado About Nothing 2.3.56-7

To be wise and love
Exceeds man's might.

Troilus and Cressida 3.2.143-4

When my love swears that
she is made of truth
I do believe her though
I know she lies.

Sonnet 138

The lunatic, the lover
and the poet
Are of imagination
all compact.

A Midsummer Night's Dream 5.1.7-8

I know no ways to mince it in
love, but directly to say
'I love you.'

Henry V 5.2.125-6

You have witchcraft
in your lips.

Henry V 5.2.256

In Shakespeare's time, plays were always performed in the afternoon as there was no artifical lighting.

Careless lust stirs up a
desperate courage,
Planting oblivion,
beating reason back.

Venus and Adonis 556-7

His unkindness
may defeat my life,
But never taint my love.

Othello 4.2.163-5

If music be the food of love,
play on.

Twelfth Night 1.1.1

Or as one nail by strength
drives out another,
So the remembrance
of my former love
Is by a newer object
quite forgotten.

The Two Gentlemen of Verona 2.4.186-8

He was more
over-shoes in love.

The Two Gentlemen of Verona 1.1.23-4

I love you more than words
can wield the matter,
Dearer than eyesight, space,
and liberty.

King Lear 1.1.53-4

I had rather hear my dog
bark at a crow than a man
swear he loves me.

Much Ado About Nothing 1.1.108-9

How wayward is
this foolish love
That, like a testy babe
will scratch the nurse
And presently, all humbled,
kiss the rod.

The Two Gentlemen of Verona 1.2.57-9

Excellent wretch! Perdition catch my soul
But I do love thee, and when I
love thee not,
Chaos is come again.

Othello 3.3.92-4

Your virginity, your old
virginity, is like one of our
French withered pears:
it looks ill, it eats drily.

All's Well That Ends Well 1.1.147-9

The word 'sex' in the
work of Shakespeare
refers only to gender.

That's a fair thought to lie
between a maid's legs.

Hamlet 3.2.107

Jacques: What
stature is she of?

Orlando: Just as
high as my heart.

As You Like It 3.2.46-7

My five wits, nor
my five senses can
Dissuade one foolish heart
from serving thee.

Sonnet 141

For your brother and my sister
no sooner met, but they
looked; no sooner looked, but
they loved; no sooner loved,
but they sighed; no sooner
sighed, but they asked one
another the reason; no sooner
knew the reason, but they
sought the remedy.

As You Like It 5.2.28-32

Kiss me, Kate, we shall be married o' Sunday.

The Taming of the Shrew 2.1.316

And then the lover,
Sighing like a furnace,
with a woeful ballad
Made to his mistress' eyebrow.

As You Like It 2.7.146-8

Lovers ever run
before the clock.

The Merchant of Venice 2.6.4

Love is blind, and
lovers cannot see
The pretty follies that
themselves commit.

The Merchant of Venice 2.6.36-7

Her passions are made of
nothing but the finest
part of pure love.

Antony and Cleopatra 1.2.133-4

Lovers can see to do
their amorous rites
By their own beauties.

Romeo and Juliet 3.2.8-9

The course of true love
never did run smooth.

A Midsummer Night's Dream 1.1.134

By heaven, I do love; and it
hath taught me to rhyme and
to be melancholy.

Love's Labour's Lost 4.3.10-11

Lovers break not hours,
Unless it be to come before
their time.

The Two Gentlemen of Verona 5.1.4-5

She's beautiful, and
therefore to be wooed;
She is a woman, and
therefore to be won.

1 Henry VI 5.5.34–5

Shakespeare's marriage does not appear to have been particularly happy as he lived most of his life in London while Anne seems to have stayed in Stratford.

It is as easy to count
atomies as to resolve the
propositions of a lover.

As You Like It 3.2.211-2

This is the very ecstasy of love,
Whose violent
property fordoes itself
And leads the will
to desperate undertakings.

Hamlet 2.1.103-5

What light is light,
if Silvia be not seen?
What joy is joy,
if Silvia be not by?

The Two Gentlemen of Verona 3.1.174-5

Your daughter and the Moor
are now making the beast
with two backs.

Othello 1.1.117-8

Virginity is peevish, proud, idle, made of self-love which is the most inhibited sin in the canon. Keep it not.

All's Well That Ends Well 1.1.134-6

This woman's an easy
glove, my lord, she goes off
and on at pleasure.

All's Well That Ends Well 5.3.274-5

Misery acquaints a man
with strange bedfellows.

The Tempest 2.2.36-7

Virginity breeds mites,
much like a cheese...

All's Well That Ends Well 1.1.32-3

Lechery, lechery, still
wars and lechery!
Nothing else holds fashion.

Troilus and Cressida 5.2.193-4

The horn, the horn,
the lusty horn
Is not a thing
to laugh to scorn.

As You Like It 4.2.18-9

They are in the very wrath of
love, and they will together.
Clubs cannot part them.

As You Like It 5.2.35-6

So lust, though to a
radiant angel linked,
Will sate itself in a
celestial bed,
And prey on garbage.

Hamlet 1.5.55-7

Who ever loved that
loved not at first sight?

As You Like It 3.5.83

I know a lady in Venice
would have walked
barefoot to Palestine for a
touch of his nether lip.

Othello 4.3.36-7

There's no bottom, none,
In my voluptuousness. Your
wives, your daughters,
your matrons, and your maids,
could not fill up
The cistern of my lust.

Macbeth 4.3.61-4

Even now, now, very now,
an old black ram
Is tupping your white ewe.

Othello 1.1.88-9

Mistress, know yourself;
down on your knees
And thank heaven, fasting,
for a good man's love.

As You Like It 3.5.58-9

They say all lovers swear more performance than they are able, and yet reserve an ability that they never perform.

Troilus and Cressida 3.2.78-9

Love comforteth like
sunshine after rain,
But lust's effect is
tempest after sun.
Love's gentle spring doth
always fresh remain,
Lust's winter comes 'ere
summer half be done.
Love surfeits not, lust
like a glutton dies.
Love is all truth, lust
full of forged lies.

Venus and Adonis 799-804

The sea hath bounds,
but deep desire hath none.

Venus and Adonis 389

Shakespeare owned the second largest house in Stratford. He bought this house called 'New Place' for £60 in 1597.

He ... wears her like
her medal, hanging
About his neck.

The Winter's Tale 1.2.309-10

Groping for trouts
in a peculiar river.

Measure for Measure 1.2.80

There's beggary in the
love that can be reckoned.

Antony and Cleopatra 1.1.15

You rise to play and
go to bed to work.

Othello 2.1.118

Is it not strange that
desire should so many
years outlive performance?

2 Henry IV 2.4.234-5

The sight of lovers
feedeth those in love.

As You Like It 3.4.51

For thy sweet love
remembered such
wealth brings
That then I scorn to change
my state with kings.

Sonnet 29

Cupid is a knavish lad
Thus to make poor
females mad.

Midsummer Night's Dream 3.3.28-9

Shakespeare was
an actor as well
as a writer.

Speak low if you speak love

Much Ado About Nothing 2.1.82-3

She loved me for the
dangers I had passed
And I loved her that
she did pity them.

Othello 1.3.166-7

Loving goes by haps:
Some Cupid kills with arrows,
some with traps.

Much Ado About Nothing 3.1.106-7

This bud of love by
summer's ripening breath
May prove a beauteous
flower when next we meet.

Romeo and Juliet 2.1.163-4

Is love a tender thing?
It is too rough,
Too rude, too boist'rous,
and it pricks like thorn.

Romeo and Juliet 1.4.25-6

Let every eye
negotiate for itself,
And trust no agent;
for beauty is a witch
Against whose charms
faith melteth into blood.

Much Ado About Nothing 2.1.156-8

Let me not to the
marriage of true minds
Admit impediments.

Sonnet 116

She made great Caesar
lay his sword to bed.
He ploughed her,
and she cropped.

Antony and Cleopatra 2.2.233

Love is too young to know
what conscience is.

Sonnet 151

Men's vows are
women's traitors.

Cymbeline 3.4.53

Love will not be spurred
to what it loathes.

The Two Gentlemen of Verona 5.2.7

What did he when thou sawest him? What said he? How looked he? Wherein went he? What makes he here? Did he ask for me? Where remains he? How parted he with thee? And when shalt thou see him again? Answer me in one word.

As You Like It 3.2.201-4

Love looks not with the eyes,
but with the mind,
And therefore is winged
Cupid painted blind.

A Midsummer Night's Dream 1.1.234-35

O know, sweet love,
I always write of you,
And you and love are
still my argument.

Sonnet 76

My bounty is as
boundless as the sea,
My love as deep.
The more I give to thee
The more I have, for
both are infinite.

Romeo and Juliet 2.1.175-7

To live
In the rank sweat of an
enseamed bed,
Stewed in corruption,
honeying and making love
Over the nasty sty!

Hamlet 3.4.81-4

Love hath made
thee a tame snake.

As You Like It 4.3.69-70

You draw me, you
hard-hearted adamant.

A Midsummer Night's Dream 2.1.195

Love and constancy is dead.

The Phoenix and Turtle 22

Shakespeare was 18 and his wife Anne 26 when they were married in November 1852. She was also three months pregnant.

Who taught thee how to
make me love thee more,
The more I hear and
see just cause of hate?

Sonnet 150

Weigh what loss your
honour may sustain
If with too credent ear
you list his songs,
Or lose your heart, or
your chaste treasure open
To his unmastered
importunity.

Hamlet 1.3.29-32

She would hang on him
As if increase of
appetite had grown
By what it fed on.

Hamlet 1.2.143-5

I will not be sworn but
love may transform me
to an oyster.

Much Ado About Nothing 2.3.21-2

In thy youth thou wast
as true a lover
As ever sighed upon
a midnight pillow.

As You Like It 2.4.21-2

O beauty,
Till now I never knew thee.

Henry VIII 1.4.76-7

What love can do,
that dares love attempt.

Romeo and Juliet 2.1.110

He capers nimbly
in a lady's chamber
To the lasivicious
soundings of a lute.

Richard III 1.1.12

Keep within the
rear of your affection,
Out of the shot and
danger of desire.
The chariest maid
is prodigal enough
If she unmask her
beauty to the moon.

Hamlet 1.3.34-7

Hear my soul speak.
The very instant that
I saw you, did
My heart fly to
your service.

The Tempest 3.1.63-5

Doth not the appetite alter?
A man loves the meat in his
youth that he cannot endure
in his age.

Much Ado About Nothing 2.3.10-11

Love is begun by time,
And Time qualifies the
spark and fire of it.

Hamlet 4.7.93-5

Women attended theatre performances, but often wore masks to conceal their identity.

Let thy love be
younger than thyself,
Or thy affection
cannot hold the bent.

Twelfth Night 2.4.35-6

Adieu, valour! rust, rapier!
be still, drum! for your
manager is in love.

Love's Labour's Lost 1.2.160–1

Moreover, urge
his hateful luxury
And bestial appetite
in change of lust,
Which stretched unto their
servants, daughters, wives.
Even where is raging eye,
or savage heart,
Without control, listed
to make prey.

Richard III 1.1.12

Love is merely a madness, and
I tell you, deserves as well a
dark house and a whip as
madmen do.

As You Like It, 3.2.359-60

The stroke of death is
as a lover's pinch,
Which hurts and is desired.

Antony and Cleopatra 5.2.286-7

We that are
true lovers run into
strange capers.

As You Like It 2.4.47-8

Is this the generation of love?
Hot blood, hot thoughts,
and hot deeds? Why, they
are vipers. Is love a
generation of vipers?

Troilus and Cressida 3.1.122-4

This is the monstruosity in love, lady – that the will is infinite and the execution confined; that the desire is boundless and the act a slave to limit.

Troilus and Cressida 3.2.75-7

'Twere all one
That I should love a
bright particular star
And think to wed it,
he is so above me.

All's Well That Ends Well 1.1.80-2

A heart to love, and
in that heart
Courage, to make's
love known.

Macbeth 2.3.114-5

London's first proper theatre was called The Theatre and was built in Shoreditch in 1576. Before this, plays were performed in the courtyard of inns.

It is not politic in the
commonwealth of nature
to preserve virginity.

All's Well That Ends Well 1.1.119-20

O, how this spring
of love resembleth
The uncertain glory of
an April day,
Which now shows all
the beauty of the sun,
And by and by a cloud
takes all away.

The Two Gentlemen of Verona 1.3.84-7

Her passions are made
of nothing but the finest
part of pure love.

Antony and Cleopatra 1.2.133-4

Didst thou but know
the only touch of love,
Thou wouldst as soon
As seek to quench the fire of
love with words.

The Two Gentlemen of Verona 2.7.18-20

So holy and so
perfect is my love,
And I insuch a
poverty of grace,
That I shall think it
a most plenteous crop
To glean the broken
ears after the man
That the main harvest
reaps: loose now and then
A scatter'd smile and
that I'll live upon.

As You Like It

Were kisses all the joys in bed,
One woman would another wed.

The Passionate Pilgrim

On the Elizabethan stage, female characters were played by boys or by young men.

Men are April when they woo
And December when they wed.

As You Like It 4.1.139-40

O, how this spring
of love resembleth
The uncertain glory
of an April day,
Which now shows all
the beauty of the sun,
And by and by a cloud
takes all away.

The Two Gentlemen of Verona 1.3.84-7

Look out for other Prion
miniature titles:

The Languid Goat is Always Thin

Do Unto Others

Shakespeare on ...
Foreigners
Food and Drink
Doctors and Lawyers